The Truth Is. . .

MONIQUE ANTOINETTE

iUniverse, Inc.
Bloomington

The Truth Is...

iUniverse books may be ordered through booksellers or by contacting:

iUniverse
1663 Liberty Drive
Bloomington, IN 47403
www.iuniverse.com
1-800-Authors (1-800-288-4677)

Because of the dynamic nature of the Internet, any web addresses or links contained in this book may have changed since publication and may no longer be valid. The views expressed in this work are solely those of the author and do not necessarily reflect the views of the publisher, and the publisher hereby disclaims any responsibility for them.

Any people depicted in stock imagery provided by Thinkstock are models, and such images are being used for illustrative purposes only.

Certain stock imagery © Thinkstock.

ISBN: 978-1-4620-1643-3 (sc)
ISBN: 978-1-4620-1644-0 (ebook)

Printed in the United States of America

iUniverse rev. date: 7/14/2011

Acknowledgments

Thank you God for being an awesome Father; and using me to minister to people in this special way. Also, thank you for my earthly parents, brothers, sisters, sister-in-law, my nieces and nephew, my aunts, uncles, and cousins -I love y'all

And to Tim Ballany, Sheri, Charles, Cathy Serbousek, Jeremy Horn, Brad Markus, and TeYoJe Thanks for being my true friends

Contents

Mirror, Mirror

Mirror, mirror
I can't look at you
Cause if I do
I know, I would see
All da pain in me
In my eyes
All da tear stains
On my face
My dad's face
Cause everybody tells me
I look just like him
And that's kinda scary
Cause maybe I might be
Angry, like he was
When I was growing up
Not knowing when
He was going to blow up
About something that happened
In da past
And I was too scared to ask
Dad why are you so violent?
Or rather,
Who or what, made you this way?
What was your childhood like?
Is it cause of what you witnessed in the military?
Is it hereditary?
I mean
It seemed to be
No in between to me
He went from playful
To hateful
I'm talking
Zero to sixty
And on top of that
I'm not walking
I'm in a wheelchair

And so da only time I look at you
Is to brush my teeth
And do my hair

Who Am I (What Am I)

Who am I?
I'm still tryin' to figure out
But
I do know I'm a woman
Who has doubts
And insecurities
Due to my body
And society
Lookin' at me
Like I chose to be
Like this
Like I should not have been born
Like I'm a sideshow
Who's gettin' ready to perform
So my heart is a little Luke-warm
Towards da world
Sometimes
And sometimes
I feel like sayin'
Kiss my butt
But
What would that show?
A person that I wouldn't
Wanna get to know
And so
That would defeat da purpose
And I do have a purpose
For bein' here
I'm just not exactly clear
Of who
Or what
That is
…Yet

I Am

I am
Frustrated
And hate it
Cause I don't
Want to be
This way
With Cerebral Palsy
But I am
Damn
And because of it
I am. . .
Angry
All of the time
And sometimes. . .
I don't give a care . .
Who gets hurt. . .
By my mood swing
Cause it's not fair
That
My body doesn't work
Like it should
So I am depressed
About da way
I have to be
Everyday
I just
Am
And I pray
That if
There is
A tomorrow
For me
To see
Then I would be
Okay
Cause today

I
Am
Not

Created

We have created
A hypocritical
World
A stereotypical
World
We have
Become mesmerized
And hypnotized
By da diamonds
And pearls
We are poisonin'
Our boys and girls
With some of da stuff
We have exposed them to
But that's not what
God created us to do
That's not His plan
That's da devil's man
And man he is smilin'
Cause we've been wild `n' out
And we've seem to forgotten
What God's plans is for us
And that's not a plus
Cause we've created
A monster

I'm Grieving

I'm grieving
For the murdered
I'm grieving
For the missing
I'm grieving
For those
Who were suppose
To be paying attention
And not to mention
Tell the law
What they saw
We're in Hell
And it's our fault
We're still caught up
In celebrities
To protect our babies
It's crazy
But true
We need to do
Something
We need to pray
For peace
And
Guidance
To bring an end
To all this violence
All over the world
Against our boys
And girls
Against our brothers
And sisters
Against our mothers
And daughters
Because it's my belief
Since we caused
This grief

We should
End it

How I Really Feel Today (July 6, 2003)

My hormones. . .
Are raging like a 15 year old
I need God. . .
To have mercy on my soul
Because today I really want to flex. . .
My sexual muscle
You know. . .
Be some guys' girl tonight
Let him rock my world tonight
Just make me feel dynamite
I know it's not right. . .
To feel this way
But I have to keep it real
I do
Today
And I just can't say. . .
Go away like we do the rain
But I'm in pain
I feel so ashamed
There's no one to blame
It's just is. . .
What it is
Another yearning sensation
For me
Another temptation
For me
And just too much information
For you

I Feel So Much

I Feel
Like a burden
For everyone
It would've been easier
If I was a son
I got cut off at da pass
Cerebral Palsy is a pain in da ass
It's insane, how angry I am
And I don't give a damn
Who knows it
This life
I didn't choose it
I'm `bout to lose it
I feel like da biggest bitch
But I can't seem to find
The off switch
In my mind
I'm a stranger
To myself
And a danger
To others
Not even my mother
Nor my brothers are safe
From my frustration
My hater-ration
That they can walk
And I can't
Now I ain't saying
That I wish
"THIS"
On them now
I'm just pissed
`Cause I don't know how
Much more I can take
I feel like. . .
I goin' to have a nervous breakdown

The Womb

I wish I could
Go back into
The womb
So I would
Be safe
From all of
"This" social harm
Only to be kept warm
By my mother's voice
And her choice of music
'Cause right now
I'm feelin' the blues
Cause of the news
Cause of 'this' world
The suffering of others
Violence against my sistas and bruthas
Is why
I
Don't want to be
Here
At least not in "this" sense
Surrounded by fear
At least until "this" world
Started makin' sense
Would I have wanted to be a part of
"This" world
And not a minute too soon
I would've still been in. . .
The womb

Daddy's Little Girl

Even in my twenties
I yearn to be
Daddy's
Little
Girl
Treated
Like my brother
Treats his daughter
He handles his business
Emotional fo' real
He expresses how he feels
And she knows da deal
Even as a baby
And she will appreciate it
More as she grows
But as for me
I suppose
I will always be yearnin'
Always be wishin
For someone to fill that position
Unless I get a step daddy
Seriously even now
I pray for one
So late in da game
And it's a shame
How society
Doesn't see
How we
Meanin' females too
Starve for daddies to do
Their part to nurture our hearts
Just as much as guys do

My State Of Mind

I'm a female
So they say
But I don't feel like one today
Or any other day of the week
So I must be a freak
Because I am not a male
And you could tell that just by looking at me
But you couldn't tell that I am not happy
Because I hide it well
I feel like I'm in Hell
In jail
For life
Or sentenced to death
By lethal injection
When the devil shot me up with Cerebral Palsy
Which has turned guys against me
To the point of no affection
Let alone a date
I guess this is my fate
Which I hate
And that's why, I'm in a depressed state of my mind

My Body

My body
Which I hate
I wouldn't wish its physical state. . .
On another human being
And I'm not speaking sexually
I'm talking about how. . .
My body
Works for me
Or rather how it doesn't. . .
Work for me
I hate it
`Cause I didn't have a choice of being
Born this way
But I'm certain. . .
That Satan. . .
Did this to me
`Cause I'm hurtin'
In this body
And God doesn't hurt
Anybody,
Out of the startin' gate
Never has
Never will
But I still
Have to live
In this body

My Inner Child

My inner child
Keeps having nightmares
Of my parents
Getting back together
I don't know how much longer
I can weather this storm
Dreaming about things
That once had me screaming
To be taken out of this world
And even though I'm a woman now
Somehow I`m still that frightened little girl
From 1319 E. Washington Ave.
That has been through so much already
But my past is steady hunting me
Like Freddie Crooger
Taking me to those days
When I needed my teddy bear
To sleep with me at night
Along with a nightlight
I might get some sleep
Tonight
But I'm not anticipating it
It's like Satan be waiting
For my eyes to close
Then
BAM
I am
A kid again

My Superman

When we were kids, I was always amazed by the things you did. Those back flips you use to do really trip me out. As well as your illustrations. My superman. Is what I use to call you secretly to myself. Because it seemed like no one else could do what you could do. And I felt honored just to be able to spend time with you. Because you always made me feel like a queen. We did everything together. Every single day. You would come and get me so we could play. You didn't care that I was in a wheelchair. Then you moved away and we lost touch. I missed you so much. And I cried because my sidekick wasn't by my side. And I just wondered what you were up to. Then one day out of the blue, I got this "need to find you" feeling. But I didn't know why. But when I did find you, I felt whole again. I felt eight years old again. And I was ready for us to write another chapter after being apart for so long. But right away things started to go wrong. When you needed me, I was there. In fact, I was there for you too much. Because I was a friend and became a crutch . But when the shoe was on the other foot, you were nowhere to be found. You just put me down. And now I'm burning, but it's not all your fault. Because I got caught up in the way things use to be. That I couldn't see the reality. That you weren't really into me. Even though you said you was. I know now, you just said it because you needed me at the time. So you worked me. And you hurt me. But without a doubt, what we had as kids I will always treasure. And it's something that can't be measured. Or priced. I will always be grateful for that time in my life. And you will always be my superman.

Friends (Revisited)

I haven't been right
Since ya'll left me
With no explanation
No hesitation
Ya'll just left
Left me wondering
What it was I did wrong
To get left
Alone
With no one
To lean on
In times of need
Or just to have around
I haven't been quite right
Since ya'll put me down
Leaving me searching
My soul
My heart
My mind
All of this time
For the answer
When ya'll just could've told me
The truth
Even if ya'll thought it
was my fault
Ya'll should've told me
So I could've fixed myself
So I could stop getting
Left

Bitta

The truth is. . .
I'm terrified. . .
That I'm gonna wind up
Old and bitta
Cleanin up afta litta
Cause I can't seem to let go
Of how certain people have. . .
Hurt me so much
I've seemed to have lost
Touch with my happier self
Cause I keep gettin' left
Or blindsided
And I've been hidin it
Been concealing
My real feelings
I'm tired of fakin
When my heart
Is breakin
When my heart
Is achin
From all
Da trash
From my past
So I've got to get it out
In da open
`Cause I'm tired of just gettin' by
I've tried just copin'
With my hurt
Cause I still feel like dirt
So somethin' got to give
Cause I don't want to live
My life that way
I want to be somebody's wife
Someday
So I must throw
All my baggage away

And trust that my heart will
Be refilled with only sweet memories

Veronica (A.K.A Ronnie)

Ronnie,
I still miss you girl
And I know that I always will
Until I see you again "FRIEND"
Yes, you were the true definition of one
And I thank you for that
I would give anything to have you back
Physically
Even though, I do feel you spirit
Your voice, I yearn to hear it
But I know you had no choice
In leaving
But I'm still grieving
Trying to figure out
The reason for you
Not being here
And being there
But I don't care about
The lesson
I was suppose to learn
And did I learn it
"TODAY"
All I care about
Is the way
I feel
And fo' real
Girl,
I
MISS
YOU

Façade

Sometimes we didn't have lights
Sometimes we didn't have water
Sometimes we didn't have gas
Sometimes I hated my father
`Cause he was violent
And I kept silent
`Bout all that at school
Act like everythang was cool
When in fact it was not
I got teased a lot
For the clothes I wore
`Cause I didn't buy them at the store
They were hand me downs
So they wasn't "in"
And I had to pretend
That the girl who claimed to be
My best friend
All through elementary
And junior high
Didn't really make me cry
On the inside
I had to lie
No one told me to
I felt like that's what I
Had to
Do
So no one would
Suspect anything
Was wrong with me
Or at my home
`Cause sometimes my phone
Was disconnected
I felt so alone
And those were some of my darkest days
Some of my darkest hours
I don't know where

I got da power
To go on
But
Then I grew up
And found out
That I wasn't alone
The only one with a fa‡ade
There are thousands
Like me
That feel like shit
That feel like.
They have to wear
A smiley face
Just to survive
This place
And yeah it's sad
But true

There Was A Time

There was a time
In my life
When I didn't believe
In Christ

It was those times
When my daddy
Would beat my mommy
Like she was a man
I couldn't understand

If He exist
Then why in the hell
Wouldn't He tell my dad to stop?
Instead of having my little brother and I
Cry as we try to run for cover
Hoping that our mother wouldn't die

I asked why wouldn't He help?
Why was so much fear dealt?
Why was so much pain felt?

If He died so we could have a better life?
Then why did I see daddy threaten mommy with a knife?
And why was I born with Cerebral Palsy?

So many questions I would ask 'bout my past
And that lasted until I was seventeen
When CJ took me to a teen gatherin'
On a Monday
Called Young Life
That changed my life
Or rather my heart 'bout Christ
Where we sung inspirational songs
And discussed Him

Now all that was said
I had heard before
But that night
It meant more

And I started to feel
That He might be real
But there was a time
SURPRISE

I'm always surprised
When I open my eyes
I'm always surprised
When I get out of bed
`Cause so many times
Before I discovered poetry
I wished I was dead
But instead
He kept on wakin' me up
For what
I'm not totally sure
Of my purpose
Or the pain I've endured
But He does
`Cause I'm still here
With tears and fears
Even those years
When I didn't believe in Him
Those days when my life looked grim
He kept suprisin' me with the gift of life

I Don't Understand

I don't understand. . .
How many more talented
People are than me
Are dead
Or choosing to be
Crack heads
Instead
Of taking care
Of their off spring
Or bringing an end
To this sadness
This madness
Which we are living in
I can no longer pretend
That I understand
Why things are
The way they are
But I don't
I just won't
All this confusing
All this misusing
Of time
To stop
And rewind
And start doing
What we are called
To do

Backwards

We seem to be more
Concerned about animals rights
More than children's
You know that ain't right
That's backwards
And we have lost touch with reality
If you ask me
If Touched by an Angel
Got canceled
But Jerry Springer
Is still on
Now come on
That's wrong
That's backwards
And Ellen's sitcom
Got taken away
When she announced
That she was gay
But now it's okay
For straight actors
To portray characters
Who are
And now
They're considered to be superstars
That's backwards to me
And when Janet's breast was shown
Oh how I think it was totally blown out of portion
Due to the fact that I never would have known
That it happen because I blinked
But I saw it on TV every sixty seconds
And the FCC was really only pissed
At Janet Jackson but they must've missed
All the other action before her breast
Like backup dancers being half dressed
And sexually parading
For higher rating

I mean that's the real reason
MTV was hired to produce
To do the so-called family show
To get the young people fired up
But that's backwards though

Forward

I look forward
To dating you
Waiting to
Kiss you
To miss you
When you go away
On a business trip
When you slip
A ring on my finger
Asking me to be your bride
Feeling you inside of me
Giving you my virginity
And maybe
Making a baby
That night
We could
It might happen
Listen
I don't know if any of these things
Will happen between you and me
All I know is that.. .
I look forward. . .
To the possibility

I'm Lookin'

I'm lookin
for the man
to whom "this" rib
belongs to
So tell me
does "this" rib
belong to you?
`Cause I'm lookin'
for a "man"
who will see me
as his equal
I'm lookin'
for a "man"
who will see me
as his best friend
on "Earth"
who puts God first
but values my worth
So now the question is. . .
Am I the one
you're lookin' for?

.Com

I looked for love in cyberspace
But. . .
The only thing the guys wanted to know
Is how soon could they come over
To my place
And get in my bed
Before they found out
What was in my head
With no reservations
And no interest
In general conversation
But I can't lie
I was down with
A little dirty talk
And they was too
Until I mentioned that
I had a disability
Then they suddenly
Lost interest in me
I was feelin' so down
Durin' that time
All that was on my mind
Was feelin' better
And society says
Gettin' some play
Is the best way
And I was thinkin'
Maybe

A Good Book

It's me, myself, and I
In this room
Feelin'. . .
Nothin'. . .
But gloom
I wish I could. . .
Change the lyrics
To my heart song
But I can't 'cause. . .
I am
Home alone
And I feel like. . .
I don't even. . .
Belong
In this world
'Cause I'm a "keep it real" girl
Trapped in this "physically disabled"
BODY
And that's why. . .
A guy
Won't ask me out
On a date
But I didn't ask . . .
For this fate
Y'ALL ACT LIKE I. . .
LIKE MY BODY THIS WAY
NO WAY
THAT'S WHY I PRAY THAT SOMEDAY. . .
I WILL WALK. . .
WITHOUT ANY ASSISTANCE OF ANY KIND
AND TRULY I WILL SOMEDAY
BUT STILL FELLAS, IT DOESN'T MAKE ANY SENSE
TO DISCRIMININATE AGAINST ME,
ESPECIALLY SINCE I JUST MIGHT BE. . .
THE WOMAN U BEEN LOOKIN' FOR. . .
TO GIVE YOUR HEART TO. . .

THE ONE:
THAT WOULD LOVE U. . .
LIKE NO WOMAN HAS BEFORE. . .
WOULD KEEP U YEARNIN FOR MORE
MENTALLY
EMOTIONALLY
AND PHYSICALLY
BUT U DON'T EVEN WANT TO DISCOVER
SOLELY BASED ON MY BOOK'S COVER

Parental Advisories

Parental advisories
Are there
For you
Parents
To be aware
Of what your kids might be listening to
When they are not around you
And that's all the recording industry is required
By law to do
So that you want drop your jaw in shock
Just like radio stations block certain words
Out of songs
TV and Film
Rate or delete scenes
I mean,
What else do you want them to do. . .
To help you raise "your"kids?
So if you don't like what. . .
Lil' Kim or Emimem is saying,
Or like the roles that Samual L. Jackson and Denzel are playing
Then don't spend your money on them again
To watch or listen
But I am advising You to get PARENTAL
And start paying attention

Issues

I got issues
And sometimes
I need a tissue
A shoulder
To cry on
And nothing
Is wrong
With that
Because
In fact
I'm not
The only one
Trying to stay afloat
On this "Life" boat
Searching for the reason
For "this" rough Season
I'm going through
But it helps me to know
Through my issues I will grow
And become stronger
In the mind and in the heart

We Gotta Get It Togetha

Certain people are still. . .
Waitin' for Elvis. . .
Waitin' for Tupac. . .
To came back
They want so much for the theories
Surroundin' their absence to be a fact
And for their deaths to be a lie. . .
But no, not I. . .
I'm waitin'. . .
for the return. . .
OF: THE BIG GUY
Jesus Christ
The one who gave His life
For you and me
In hopes that WE. . .
Would make this world a better place. . .
Before we see His face again
Now listen, this isn't a dis
To Elvis nor Tupac
`Cause I love them too
But. . .
Time. . .
Is. . .
Runnin' out. . .
For me. . .
And for you.. .
So WE. . .
Gotta get "it" togetha
TOGETHA

No One's Perfect

I'm not perfect
But I'm worth it
This I know
Because the Bible says so
And you're not perfect
This I know
Which means that we all have room to grow
Because we have
Weaknesses. ..
Limitations
And we all have given into temptations
This has been going on for generations
But don't fret
Just let
God guide
Let Him ride beside you
In "this" the road trip of your "LIFE"
With you and your friends
So He can show you. . .
How to drive. . .
Over speed bumps,
Or help you drive in
BAD WEATHER
Because no one. . .
Can do anything. . .
Alone
Because no one's perfect

There's Something Wrong With "This" Picture

There's something wrong
With "this" picture
We are not living
By the scripture
There are people living
On streets
While athletes make boo coo money
Teachers are being under paid
And students are being held back a grade
Because our government is being ran. . .
Shady. . .
If you ask me
The world is hooked. . .
On these so-called reality TV shows
I suppose
To look after their kids development
So the state sale them
To the highest bidder
And now they're getting molested. . .
By their babysitter
Because you really didn't take a good look. . .
At the picture
"You" took
You just put it in your photo book

I Miss Those Days

I miss those days
When we use to solve our problems
By street boxing
Brake dancing
Battle rapping
What happened?
Guns
Drive bys
And homicides
Oh how I miss those days
When only your pride got hurt
And your ego was bruised
But it went no further
Then you win, you lose
Murder never came into play
But it does today
In a major way
No one just walks away
Anymore
We are at war
In da hood
And
I miss
Da good ol' dayz a lot
Cause nobody got
Carried away by the cops
Or in a body bag
And those were some of
Da best times
I ever had
And I desperately
Want them back

The Root

Spouses killing spouses
Parents killing kids
Now how did
We get here
When did our fear
Turn into anger
Anger into rage
Rage into becoming
A danger to others
And then winding
Up on the front page
A person doesn't change
Over night
Some had to be not quite right
Way before someone's feelings
Manifested into killing someone
You supposedly cared about
The whole world needs counseling
We need to talk it out
Get to the root
Of our problems
And then learn
How to solve them
RIGHT NOW
WE CAN'T WAIT
WE CAN CHANGE
OUR FATE
WE JUST NEED TO BE
IN HOT PURSUIT
OF THE ROOT

A Choice

We always have a choice
Or should I say choices
Either to stay silent
Or use our voices
To do right
Or do wrong
Get weak
Or get strong
But we no longer
Look for the best solution
We are turning to selling drugs
Stripping or prostitution
For a quick buck
We'll try our luck
At anything
Even if it seems
Like a scheme
Any means
Of making green
At
That
Time
And if it means
Committing a crime
It seems to be
Okay
Today
It seems that only crime
Pays
But that's not true
Because believe me
We always have. . .
CHOICES

We Glamorize

We glamorize
Violence
And then
We get silent
When it's acted
Out in real life
What's that about?
And we glamorize
Creeping
Sleeping
With multiple peeps
Until
HIV seeps out
Them and into us
Do we want to discuss
Abstinence
Or the importance
Of using protection
But yet and still
We are choosing
To glamorize things
That has us losing lives
Tragically
Daily
`Cause of 90 percent
Of what being portrayed
In the entertainment world
Is divided between
Gettin' sprayed
Gettin' laid
Or gettin' paid
By any means necessary
Scary
`Cause it doesn't have to be
"THIS WAY"

You Let. . .

You let someone
Kiss you
You let someone
Feel you
Inside of them
In some form
You got warm
With someone else
Besides your mate
But wait you expect them
To stay
After you did
What you did to them
When hell, you know
Damn well
You wouldn't
And you shouldn't
'Cause they could've gotten sumthin
And given it to you
HIV
Or any other
STD
And it blows my mind
How people don't see
How serious infidelity is
And how serious
It can become

If You Didn't Wanna Be A Momma

It's like you woke up one day
And decided that you just didn't want to be. . .
A momma
Anymore
My momma
Anymore
You might as well have physically thrown me out the house. . .
When you said you don't care if I never come home
But you kept your. . .
Sorry excuse for a spouse
Leaving me no other choice but. . .
To roam the street. . .
Until I got picked up by the police. . .
Or someone took me in. . .
And treated like I was their kid
After they realized what you did
You could have aborted me
Or gave me up for adoption
But you didn't. . .
Why didn't you spare me from this Trauma?
Momma

Goodbye to Your Plans

When I was in
Your tummy mommy
You said that
You would love me
Unconditionally
You said that
I could be
Anythang
I wanted to be
Until you gave birth to me
And the doctor said that
Something might be
Wrong with me
That you would have to
Just wait and see as I grew
And it turned out to be
True
And you was mad
Because you had
Big plans for me
But now,
You don't see how
I could live
The life that you
Envisioned
And now you regret your
Decision
To have me in the first place
You act like I'm a disgrace
But trust me there's a reason
For me being
Thrown into unloving clenches
I was born to help somebody else
Maybe to teach you something
About yourself
So say goodbye

To your plans
And hello to
God's

They Think, (They Don't Think)

They Think
It's okay
To pray
To You when. . .
They want to win. . .
The championship of their sport
But yet they take it out of schools
And remove Your rules. . .
The Ten Commandments
Out of courts
Then they wonder. . .
Why this world is so corrupt?
Well,
I don't have to guess
Because I know
It's because of their ignorance
But I still stress
Because it could get messier
Then it already is
And for that. . .
I'm pissed off
Because it doesn't have to be this way
But it is because. . .
They don't think

I Know

I know two guys
Two guys
That I grew up with
Who are now locked up
And SHIT
That makes me cry
On the inside
And out
`Cause it doesn't looks like. . .
They will eva get out. . .
Alive
Man, they're being deprived
A second chance
Instead. . .
They were given. . .
A song and dance
By. . .
THE SYSTEM
It's like. . .
"THEY" want to vanish them from the world
`Cause I have heard thousands of people. . .
Who have done much more heinous crimes
But yet they are not behind bars
And they didn't have to serve decades of time
Which blows my mind
`Cause if only my boys from DA HOOD. . .
Would've had some money
Th ey would've been livin'. . .
DA GOOD LIFE
Instead of servin'
DAMN NEAR LIFE

Hey, Little Run Away

Hey, little run away
I heard you wanna run da street. . .
All day and night
In clothes that are skin tight
Now, you know that aint right
`Cause some guy
Might. . .
Try to take. . .
A bite. . .
Out of your butt
He could slip you sumthin'. . .
Only God knows what
Without you knowin'. . .
Anythin' 'bout it
Until a few months later. . .
A blue line appears on a stick
And now you stuck with a child
`Cause you got buck wild
Or maybe he won't leave you with a creation
But with a burnin' sensation
And all `cause "you". . .
Had street feet
THINK ABOUT IT

Bang, Bang, Bang

Bang, bang, bang. . .
A kid falls down. . .
In his schoolyard. . .
But not in the way. . .
He fell down in his backyard. . .
When he use to play. . .
Cops and robbers. . .
Or cowboys and Indians. . .
Because you see, he's not playing. . .
He's lying down. . .
On the ground. . .
Because he's dead. . .
Dead, for real. . .
Killed, by some steel. . .
In the hands of one his peers. . .
Who was insane. . .
No, in pain. . .
Who was probably crying out way before. . .
He went in his dad's drawer. . .
But no one was there to listen. . .
No one was paying attention. . .
No one did a thing. . .
And because of that. . .
BANG, BANG, BANG

Another Kid

Another kid dies
From being left in a car
Another kid dies
From being shook
But it's like we don't care
Or realize
But we would
If we could
If we wasn't so concerned . . .
With celebrities twist and turns
Or we even seem to be. . .
More concerned with stopping animal cruelty
Which really burns me up
Make me want to throw up
How we put these things
Before. . .
Our kids
We have really fl ipped. . .
Our lids
To let things like this happen to our kids
Yes "our kids"
Because it take a village to raise a
child
So it going to take a village to save. . .
Another kid

You Killed Me

You killed me
So why isn't it killing you,
Bush
To know that
You
Pushed
Me
Into a line of fire?
And now because of You
I no longer desire
Because I'm dead
Because You lead
Me
To believe that
We
Were in this
Together
But you just sit there
Behind your big desk
In your big leather chair
And I swear
You
Don't care what
You
Did to my family
My wife
Or my kid
I tell you
It's like
You
Don't have a heart
Well I did
Until I got shot
Then it stop beating
And you say that
The war is over
NOT

America

America-who do you think you are girl? You are ruining this world. You said that the war was over. But soldiers are dying. Which means Families are still crying. Because they miss their loved ones. So you need to stop lying. We can handle the truth. If we have stuck by your side even after we knew you lied to us. But yet and still you don't trust our loyalty to you. I mean what else do we have to do to get you and Uncle Sam to divulge a top secret or two. I mean, damn we 're like Fam and all so we died for Ms. Red-White-Blue thinking that "our" main goals was to secure "our" safety and freedom. Because that's what we were told. But "your" ultimate goal must've been to our souls. So you got us to fight under false pretenses- Now that's cold Girl

Dear America

Dear America,
My name is Africa and I need to be fed (And yes, those are tear stains on the letter.) I have been crying 'cause my mommy was dying but now she dead. Died last night from something called AIDS. Have you heard of it? I haven't until now. I don't know how I'm going to make it here without her. People here say she would not have get sick so quick, if she got some medicine 'cause ain't no cure. And I'm sure missing her right now. I still don't know how she got it But don't care, because there's no one to take care of me now. Can you help me? Can I please come and live in your country? Or can you at least send me some money? Because I don't want to die this way hungry and alone with no real home. Sincerely Africa

War

Kanye West
Said it best
There are
All types
Of wars
That can
Cause all kinds
Of sores
Internally
And externally
All types could be
Fatal to you
And me
From the cradle
We learn to
Turn on each other
Just like we learn to
Pretend
We learn to
Hold stuff in
And this is how
A war starts
It digests
In our hearts
And in our spirit
But we don't listen
Or pay attention
Until someone
Throws up
Or something
Blows up

Hungry (Homeless)

You throw
Your leftovers away
But I didn't eat
Yesterday
And I didn't sleep
Last night
While you were
Tucked in tight
In your bed
On your pillow
I laid under
A weeping willow
Weeping my eyes out
Because I'm hungry
And homeless
And I know what you're thinking
I got myself in this mess
So I deserve this
And maybe I do
But my kids don't
So want you help us
Please

In The Congo

In the Congo
Woman are treated
Like animals
The men
Act like cannibals
And rape them
In front of anyone
Their husbands, their daughters,
Their sons
By the soldiers
The ones who are
Suppose to protect them
Are the same ones
Who let them down
Who turn their lives
Upside down
And their souls
Inside out
But we don't
Want to talk about it
We just want to walk away
And forget about it
And act like we don't know
What's going on
In the Congo
But wait,
That sort of thing
Can happen here too
But wait,
Women do get raped
Here everyday
And still we sleep
And keep silent
About the violence
But that makes no sense to me

So how could we be okay with it?

Sex For Sale

How much is that gurl
In da video,
Da one shakin' her tail?
Sex for sale

And how much is that guy
Doin' gyration moves on stage?
I didn't know that paid
For sex though

And also I didn't know
You needed sex to sell food
Or to sell shampoo
What is da world comin' to?

And that's why
Th e percentage
Of teen pregnancy
Is high
Cause they want
To give sex a try
But these days
You can die
Cause of da way
It's bein' promoted
Everyday

Sold

I was sold to highest bidder
I was told I was bought for sex
And nothing else
And I'm too young
To help myself
So I need you
To help me
Please
Free me
Of this
Trafficking
This prostitution
You are my solution
The answer to my prayers
The end to all my tears
I been doing this for years
And I been doing this
Since I was fi e years old

Nobody but the Devil

A mother losses her three little boys
In a house fire
And if anyone thinks it was in God's plans
Well, their brain is a liar
And three little girls world was forever changed
When their mother was shot at close range
By her estranged husband
Then he put in her in the mini van
And torched it
And then he left
After causing her BODY'S horrific death
But still you blame Him
THE MAN
WHOSE SON DIED A HORRIFIC DEATH
SO YOU AND I WOULDN'T HAVE TO
And why?
Would He have a twenty year old guy
Murdered thousands of years later
Coming out of a convenience store with a
Frito chili pie
And Columbine
You gotta be out ya mind
Hurt da kids now
God loves da kids
All His kids now
Even His grown kids now
And the Twin Towers
The Pentagon
Now, true He has the powers
But He wouldn't do it
Because He couldn't do it
Because He's not EVIL
But the DEVIL would
BECAUSE HE IS EVIL
Acts can't be done by nobody. . .
But. . .
THE DEVIL

How Many?

How many more
Do we have to
Lose to the war,
Or to the street?
Before we unite and stay
That way?
And how many more kids
Have to be molested
Or come up missing
To get US
To start
Paying
Attention?
And how many more
Earthquakes or hurricanes
Is it gonna take
To shake us up
To wake us up
Inside and make us realize
We must keep our
Eyes open
And trust in God
Because the devil
Is lurking around
To break us down
To the ground
I'm not trying to sound profound
Or anything like that
I'm just asking a question
How many more tragedies,
Before we learn
Our lesson?

The Devil's Playground

The world
Is the devil's playground
And it's fun for him to see
Us run and hide
Commit suicide
And crime
Wind-up behind bars
Addicted to
Meth
Crack
Until we are so far that
We can't find our way back
He loves that
And apparently
So do we
Cause that's what I see
In the news
We choose to be
On his side
But I don't know why
Cause he hates us
We know this
It's been proven
But yet and still
We will help him ruin our lives
And play with our kids

Testifying

Okay
Fine then
That no one wants to be. . .
My friend
Or my man
Which I still don't understand
But I still do the best I can
To stay strong
To push on
But don't get me wrong
Because on occasion I throw myself. . .
A pity party
Wishing I had some Colt 45
To get drunk
And I don't even drink
I just need an excuse to babble on about. . .
How my life stinks at that moment
And then I think:
Somebody else is having a worst day
Than me so how could I be. . .
Crying like I'm dying
I'm still alive
And that's worth testifying

For Dean

I Saw, I Heard, I Felt

They said before you left
Before you took your last breath
You saw God
Well guess what, my brother
From another mother,
I saw God too
I saw God in you
In the way you walked
Man, that solider walk you had
I heard Him when you talked
You spoke with so much passion
And so much conviction
But only now I know,
That you were just on a mission
And everything you did was part of that
Down to your kisses and hugs
I felt Him
But both of you
Will forever be
A blessing
To me

Mattie

Mattie
Even though I never met you
I will never forget you
I think about you every day
"Remember to play after every storm"
Was your favorite phrase
You were so amazing
You had no fear
You know exactly
Why you were here
And I'm glad you were
Because you inspired me
To not only face my reality
But also embrace it
So I am a much more
Open person
Because of you
Sharing what you
Went through
Everyday
So I say
Thank you
For tugging on my heart strings
And making it sing

I Remember

Oprah had a guest on
That society felt
Had done wrong
But her so-called crime
Is not what's embedded
In my mind
It's her face
And her state of mind
Which mirrored her grief
And her disbelief
And rightfully so
Because she lost her husband,
The father of her children,
Her best friend
Her hero
At ground zero
A place that should become
A memorial
If you ask me
For all the family members we
Lost that day
A memory
That plays in my mind
Just like Columbine
Or Oklahoma City
It's not pretty
But I do think about them all the time
Along with
The Challenger Columbia
And learning about the Holocaust
Man, so many lives
Have been tragically lost
And from every January
Until every December
I know that I will always
Remember

Music

Music
I don't remember da first time I heard ya
But it had to be in da womb
Cause when I came out
I was already in tune
I remember growin' up
Hearin' Teddy P,
Pattie,
Luther,
And Marvin Gaye
Bein' blown away
And thankful
Towards my mom
Fa lettin' me hear you
And who knew
That you would
Help me get through
Some of da worst times
Of my life
With your
Beautiful lyrics
And your deep rhymes
I use to fall asleep
With you every night
Until my dad said
We had to save power
I was so mad at him at first
But you came and quenched my thirst
In da shower
Cause in da shower
I could bring myself joy
By singin'
AND BOY LOOK
That's what I did
When I was kid
But you know

When Left Eye died
I was shook to da core
To da point that
I really didn't want to
Hear you anymore
Cause it was just too hard
You reminded me of how much
I was emotionally scarred
By her physical passin'
And that was askin'
Too much to listen to you
But I had no choice
Cause you were in my head
You were in my heart
You were in my voice
You are a part of me

Micah

Micah
You are
More than just my niece
You are
My sense of peace
In this crazy world
It's amazing how a little girl
Can wipe away my sorrow
Give me hope for tomorrow
I know that I was truly blessed
The day you were born
And I should've been warned
That you were going to steal my heart
Right from the start
And make me bust my butt
Tryin' to give you da world
Girl,
I love you
Like the Bible
Defines love
And I love God
And your parents
For creating you
You are truly
A dream come true
And thank you for being you

Falsely Accused

Now here I am
Been sittin' in this Cell,
Been goin' through Hell
All this time
But I didn't
Do da crime
I was Falsely Accused
I had my life,
Taken away,
My wife,
Taken away,
My kids
Taken away
From me
I've been cryin'
Like a baby
`Cause I did nothin' wrong
Been here
For years
And it look like
I'm goin' to be here
Some more
I don't wanna live
No more
What
Do
I
Have
To
Live
For?
Cause this is no life
Away from my wife
And kids
Under false pre-tenses
Locked down

Probably until…
I'm…
Under
Ground

Rehabilitation

All you wanna do
Is lock me up
With no reservations
No rehabilitation
Just lock my behind up
And it doesn't matter
If my time fits da crime
Or not
You just got
To lock me up
That's your only concern
And it doesn't matter
If I could turn my life around
You just wanna lock me down
And I'm facin' over a decade
For da mistake I made
My first strike
But you're treatin' me like
I'm a murderer
Or a rapist
Yes I know I did wrong
But I don't belong
In da same category
That's nowhere near close
To my story
But I'm in here
And they're already out
What's that about?

Yesterday, Today, And Tomorrow

Yesterday I was sad
Yesterday I was mad
Yesterday I just wanted
The pain to stop
And I just wanted to scream
At the top
Of my lungs
But that was yesterday
But today
I wanna live
And give
In any way
I can
To help
My fellow man
And
I look forward
To tomorrow

Some People

Some people
Are never satisfied
Some people
Just wanna run and hide
Commit suicide
And that's sad to say
But what's sadder is
I use to be that way
But it doesn't mater
Cause I don't feel that way anymore
But some people still do
And maybe I was created to
Help some people
Get to the place
I am at in my life
At peace
But
It's all because of
Christ

A Change In Me

So many thoughts
Run through my head
But I no longer wish
That I was dead
Instead
I wanna live and give
Back to others
And in fact I don't
Even yearn for a man
To be a part of my life
Since I fully let Christ
In my heart
That day I started
To feel a change
In me
For real
I suddenly
Wanted to be
Different
To do better
For Him
In every way
I just want to
Obey
His beliefs
Because He has brought
So much peace
And given me
So many blessings
And I am forever
Grateful
And I am forever
Changed

God, I Know Now

God, I know now
That You are the answer
With no questions
You forgave me
For all of my past transgressions
With You there's no second guessing
Because You always tell me truth
So that's proof, You are my best friend
And when I put Your Words to action
In my life only good things happen
And I thank You,
As well as praise You
For that
In fact,
No one loves me
More than You do
And it trips me out
How You are working
Through me
But You can see
That it does
Because
You have seen it all
And that's why
I was surprised
When I was called
To write
In hopes that I might
Save someone else
From their selves
But I could not
Or rather would not
Listen
Or pay attention
To Your vision
Then

But I will
Now
From this day forward

My Father

For years
I have cried tears
Over my father here,
The one who introduced me to fear
But now,
That I know
My Heavenly Father
There's no real reason
To cry over that situation
Anymore
Because I am
GOD'S CREATION
And He only has
Good things in store
For me
But I was blind
So I couldn't see
How much He is
For me
How much he
Adores me
He loves me
More than my mother does
And that's hard to believe
Because she loves me a lot
But I got proof
I got "THE TRUTH"
In His autobiography
He wrote especially
For me
His daughter
And I am so honored
To be that

My Brother

My brother
Is Jesus Christ
Wow
And He died
So I could
Have eternal
Life
Oh, what a miraculous gift
That was
Because
He was
Sinless
But He did it anyway
He let "them"
Just nail Him
Because He trusted
Our Father completely
That everything
Was going to be okay
And it was
Because
He rose again
Because He chose
To obey
Our Father
So I have to say
Thank you
My brother

My Ultimate Prayer

Heavenly Father,
I pray for peace on Earth
For everybody
To realize their worth
Their gift to help
Someone else grow
Spiritually,
Mentally,
Emotionally
However
You know
So that we could
Then bond together
To change the world
For the better
Forever
This is my prayer
For I pray this
In Jesus name
Amen

Love

Love
I was lookin' for you
In all da wrong places
In peoples' faces
Mostly guys
While in visualizing
A church steeple
Not realizing
That you were
With me
All da time
Love
You are
A precious gift
From my daddy
Up above
And I will cherish You
In any form
That you come in
Whether it be
In the shape of
A husband
Or a friend
Because
Any type of love
Is good
Because
Love is God

Spoken Word

A spoken word
Has so much power
For instance
God spoke a lot of things
Into existence
Like light
Sight
Day
Night
And rain
From Genesis
To Revelations
But He also gave
This power
To His greatest creation
Us
And trust
It does work
Words can hurt
Or heal
Change
Our whole situation
For the better
Better than a pill can
And
We must understand
That we were given
Free will to move forward
And live
Or be still
And the key
To unlocking our destiny
Is to be
Careful how we speak
To each other
As well as…
Ourselves

Actions

Actions
Speak louder than words
Haven't you heard
That phrase before?
Well I had
But now it means
So much more
Because God loves
And He shows me
In every way
Every day
So if I say
That I love Him
Then I should show him
In every way
Every day
By reading
His word
And putting it to action
In my life
That He
Gave me

The N Word

I watched Oprah yesterday
And listened to what she
And the cast of Crash
Had to say about the N word
So I started to write
Down my two cents about the word
That means ignorant
Or friend
Depending on the SPELLING
And I'm telling you
I usually do say it
When it's in a song
But afterwards
I do feel like
I've done something wrong
Then images like
Emmet Till
Flash in my mind
And those girls that burned up
In that church
Because of THE N WORD
Then my stomach starts to turn
So I guess I learned a lesson
Which is always to
Listen to my gut

Looks

Looks
We put too much
Emphasis on You
Your eyes
Your chest
Your butt
Now what
Does that have to do with anything?
That doesn't tell me what
You would bring
To the table
Or how You
Could enrich someone's life
But we have let society
Cut us with a knife
Sometimes
More than twice
So we could LOOK
NICE
For a mate we haven't met yet
But wait
How do our insides
Look?

For the hurricane survivors

Survivor

Survivor
My heart goes out to you
Because of everything
You have been through
You were caught by surprise
But you will rise again
Just like the Phoenix
Because you are a survivor
But it's okay if you
Need a Kleenex
A shoulder
Someone
To hold you
Help you deal with
Your new reality
That wasn't mad for TV
But I watched
You sleep on cots
But not by choice
And then
I heard a voice
Say "Do unto others
As you would have them
Do unto you"
Why?
One, because
It's the right thing to do
And two, it could've easily
Happened to you
But wait,
It has
But not in this form of a storm
All that matters is
We survived

I Was Just Thinkin'

I was just thinkin'
How blessed I am
To be still here
With no fear
Even though the devil
Is constantly ringin'
In my ear
Tryin' to destroy me
Take my joy
By any means necessary
And I must admit
That some shit
In my life got very scary
At times
But I am still risin'
And shinin'
And growin'
Up
And showin'
Up
Everyday
To play ball
And man
When I think` bout
All I have been through
I just have to. . .
Thank You
Father

I Use To

I use to
Put so much
Trust in man
But I didn't understand
How much strife
Was going to
Enter my life
And try
To destroy the very essence
Of me
And so rapidly
Because I didn't know
That only with God
I will prosper and grow
With the help of his people
But He is the main source
Of my prosperity
In all honesty
He is the driving force
In me
My security
And without Him
My life would be
In shambles
Just like…
It use to be

Use Me

So many people
Have used me
I now see
The wrong way
But God,
He Made me
To be a living testimony
Every day
In every way
But only for good things
I am meant
I was sent
I was made
And Jesus paid
"THE ULTIMATE PRICE"
For the spread of
"THE GOOD NEWS"
And that's the only way
We're supposed to be
Used

The Truth Is. . .

The truth is
God is real
And He is good
And this is not just a feeling I have
He is something
I know from reading The Bible
Which is food to the soul
Armor against the Devil
Who is also real
Whose only motive is to. . .
KILL, STEAL, AND DESTOY
Oh yes,
Satan is waiting
To fill our brains with crazy thoughts
To get us caught up
Playing the doubt game,
The blame game,
And the shame game
Until we go insane
Or stop trying
And end up
Dying
In some form
By some storm
Because he is a Reject
The total OPPOSITE
Of the Father
And he is bothered
By the fact that he messed up
And his blessings
Were taken back
And he wants to distract us
From the only Spirit
We can truly trust
With our whole heart
From start

'Til finish

My Mission

I express myself
Until there's nothing left
Inside of me
Totally empty
But not just for my benefit
Do I share my reality
My testimony
My transgressions
My life's lessons
But this is not
My profession
This is my Mission
To get you to listen
To pay attention
To your inner voice
Your choice
Your mission
If you choose
To accept it
We all have a calling
A purpose
That is bigger than you and me
It's about
The Almighty

A Victim

Everyone needs to stop acting like a victim
And yes, I am including myself
Because I have been known
To blame someone else
For the chances "I've" blown
But I am grown
Enough, to make my own decisions
Despite my circumstances
If no one put a GUN to "my" head
And said if I move FORWARD in "my" life
Then I would be dead
No, that didn't happen
Because I am still here
But I WAS threatened by FEAR
And I am sure he threatened you too
But it doesn't matter now
Because all that matters is. . .
What are we going to do now?
How are we going to use our voices?
When are we going to take responsibility for our own choices?
And when are we going to stop acting like. . .
A VICTIM?

The Solution

I am a work in progress
You are a work in progress
Meaning there's always room for improvement
So let's start a movement
And change:
The way we are thinking
Right now
The way we are feeling
Right now
The way we are talking
Right now
The way we are walking
You know, the way we are living our lives
Right now
But how do we start?
You ask:
You just have to invite Christ
In your life and He will help us
Take care of the rest
For the rest
Of our lives

There's No Reason

There's no reason
For anyone of us
To be greedy
When there's so many
Needy
People in the world
To want more
Diamonds and pearls
When there are
So many boys and girls
Who don't have any clothes at all
Let alone
A place to call home
While you
Have a mansion
Riding in a Phantom
And have a few more
Cars in your driveway
Make someone's day
Let alone change someone's life
You have more than enough stuff now
And I just don't see how
You don't care to share
What you have been
Blessed with

I Can't Complain

I can't complain
Because as I speak
People are sleeping
On the street
Searching
For something
To eat
And trying
To keep
Warm
I`ve never been through
That bad of a storm
But I can visualize
The pain in their eyes
And I realize
I Can't Complain

I Can't Complain
Because
I'm not lying in a pool of blood
Dying
Crying out for help
But somebody is
As I speak
And I can rest my head
In a bed
And I'm clothed and fed
So I'm not even hungry
I'm not even lonely
Or depressed
Anymore
I'm not fighting in the war
I'm safe and free
I'm not anxiously
Waiting
To be paroled

You see I told ya
I Can't Complain
And chances are
You Can't Either
Not honestly

I Surrender

Just when I think I've gotten over something
Turns out I have not, but I know I got to
So I can truly serve You Father
You see, I am still bothered
By my past,
And the smallest things tend to get on my nerves
Which really disturbs me
Because this shouldn't be happening,
But those old emotions
Keep creeping up on me
So can You please
Help me calm my ocean
Of waves
Daddy
Save me from myself
Because I almost have no strength left
Trying to handle everything by myself
But I know that's what I get
For not surrendering all to You
But here and now I do
Because I know
That Your word is truth
So teach me
To be more like You
Because I wanna know
I wanna Grow
So I can serve you better
Answer Your calling
For me
I'm tired of falling
Into the same old traps
I have learned my lesson
This time I rewind
And start over
So I Surrender

I Forgive You

Here and now
I forgive you
For all of the pain
You all put me through
But truth be told,
I thought I had,
But sadly I must confess
I just suppressed
All that mess
Inside of me
Then became a slave
To my wave of emotions
And in fact
I held myself back
And I caused myself more pain
Just as much as y'all did
But I've been drowning
Since I was a kid
But I wanna live
So I must forgive
You and me
According to
The Almighty
So I can officially
Let my past rest
So God can truly bless
Us all

I Was

I was
A messed up kid
Then I became
A messed up woman
Ashamed of the things I did
And the things I said
I even felt like things would be
Better for me
And my Family
If I was dead
I mean
I was hurting in ways
I still to this day cannot express
How much I was searching
For any type of painkiller
Of any kind
Whether it be from pills
Or mankind
To take me out of my thriller
And just thinking about those days now
It gives me the chills
Because I was like a Hamster
Spinning
Round and round
On its wheel but God
Made me be still
And get real with myself
And all that left of the person I Was
Are memories
And my body

It's Morning Time

It's morning time
And I love it
Why?
`Cause the sun is shining?
No, cause I'm a part of it
A lot have passed away
But I woke up today
So I gotta say
Thank You God
Because I woke up this Morning
Yawning
And stretching
What a blessing
This is to me
Cause I lived
To see this Morning
And you did too
So Congratulations to you
Now what are we gonna do
With this Morning?
That is the question

Mirror, Mirror (Revisited)

Mirror, mirror
I can finally look at you
And see past my pain
My shame
In me
I see Beauty
I see Strength
As well as
My emotional scars
The invisible bars
I have been behind
For so long
Now I'm Strong
Enough to look at you
Still shaken up
By what I went through
In my past
But at last
I'm not afraid
About what I
Might see
When I Look at You
And You look at me
I'm Free
Of that Insecurity

About the Author

I have lived in Arkansas for most of my life. And shortly after I graduated from North Little Rock West Campus in 1997, I enrolled both in Poetry.com and Institute of Children's Literature corresponding courses proudly received diplomas 2001.